MW01014882

What's Inside?

Lurking in the Ocean

Sharks live in all of the world's oceans. Some kinds swim near the surface of the water while others lurk on the ocean floor. Sharks come in all shapes and sizes, from tiny fish that you hardly notice to giants bigger than a bus!

A mako shark is the fastest shark of all!

This strange-looking shark is called a wobbegong.

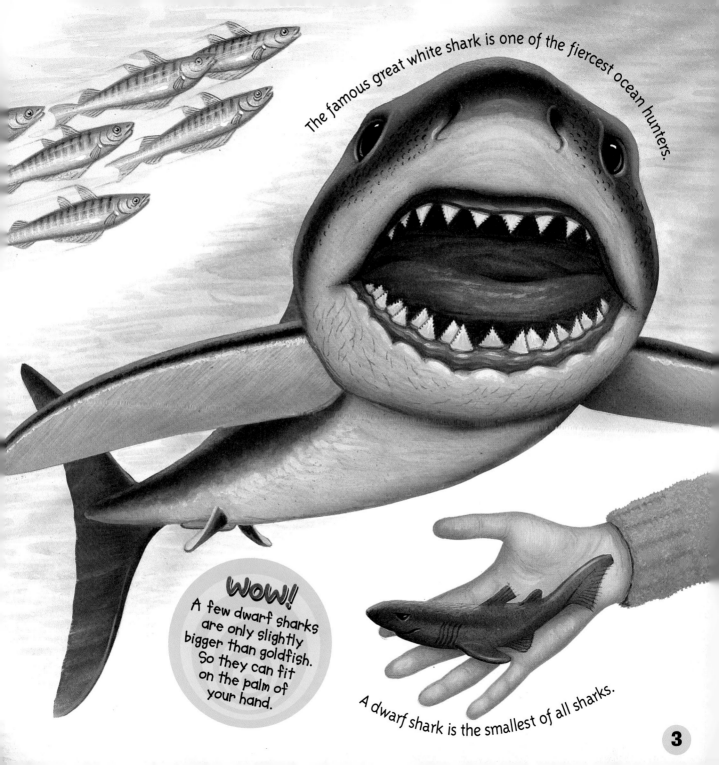

The famous great white shark is one of the fiercest ocean hunters.

WOW!
A few dwarf sharks are only slightly bigger than goldfish. So they can fit on the palm of your hand.

A dwarf shark is the smallest of all sharks.

Reef Shark

A reef shark usually hunts at night. It glides along a coral reef, looking for tasty fish to snap up for its dinner. Like all sharks, a reef shark can't just float in the water. It has to keep on swimming. Otherwise, it will slowly sink to the ocean floor!

It's a Laugh!
Why is a shark easy to weigh? Because it has its own scales!

✳ Like most sharks, a white-tip reef shark only stops swimming when it rests. It dozes in a cave on the seabed until it is ready to come out for dinner.

✳ When a gray reef shark nods its head and arches its back, it's time to move. The shark is about to attack.

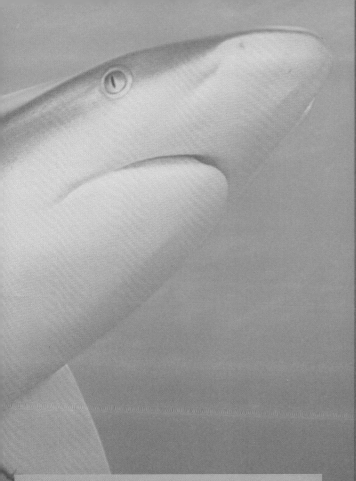

Q Is a shark as smooth as it looks?

A No! A shark looks smooth, but actually its skin is covered with rough scales that protect the fish like a suit of armor. If you were to stroke a shark, it would hurt your hand.

Ouch!

✳ A reef shark is a handy scrubbing brush for a rainbow runner fish. The tiny fish rubs itself against the shark's rough skin to make itself sparkly and clean.

On the Hunt

Sharks are powerful hunters. They can see and hear extremely well and have an excellent sense of smell to help them track down animals to eat. Sharks race toward their prey, steering with their tails. Then they open their mouths and bite hard!

Can You Believe It?

A shark's sense of smell is about 2,000 times more powerful than yours! This comes in handy at dinnertime. At the first whiff of blood, the shark just zooms off to find its prey.

I'm done for!

◀ Stunning Tail

A thresher shark has a magnificent tail as long as its body. It uses its tail like a whip to stun fish and herd them together.

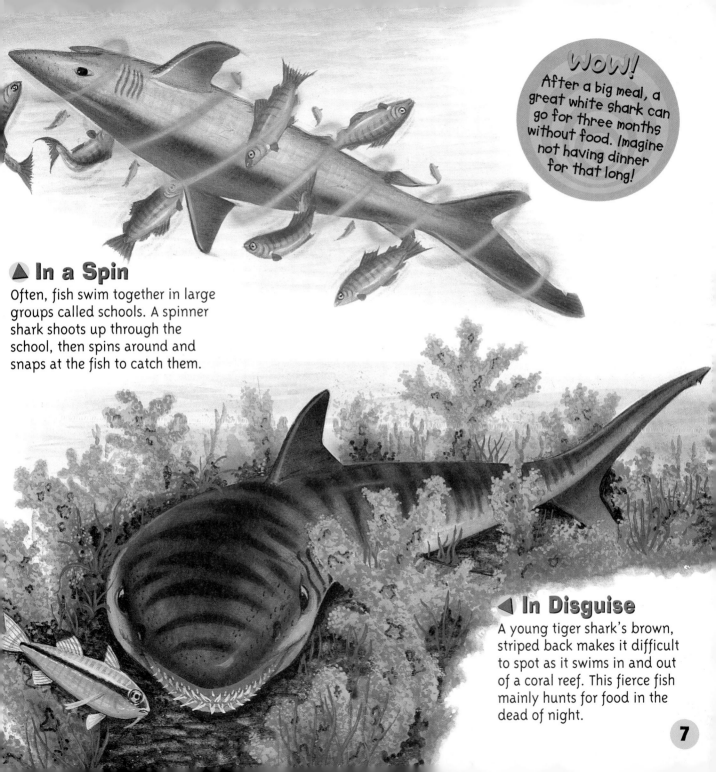

▲ In a Spin

Often, fish swim together in large groups called schools. A spinner shark shoots up through the school, then spins around and snaps at the fish to catch them.

◀ In Disguise

A young tiger shark's brown, striped back makes it difficult to spot as it swims in and out of a coral reef. This fierce fish mainly hunts for food in the dead of night.

7

Mako Shark

A mako shark has rows of sharp teeth shaped like needles to catch slippery fish. Its favorite meal is swordfish, which it snaps up in its teeth, then swallows whole. This strong, fierce shark is one of the fastest swimmers in the sea.

It's a Laugh!
Why are sharks like chalkboards? Because they are found in schools!

Q **Why do sharks lose their teeth?**

A Sharks often lose teeth when they bite into their prey. But they don't need to worry. New teeth are constantly growing and just move forward to take the place of the old ones.

A mako shark can zoom through the water at up to 20 miles (32 kilometers) per hour. That's four times faster than an Olympic swimmer.

Watch out! When a mako shark leaps out of the water, it can jump higher than a sail on a sailboat.

When a mako shark feels threatened, it may bite a boat so hard that it leaves its teeth behind.

Feeding Time

Sharks feast on all kinds of tasty food. Some sharks snap up large animals, including seals, penguins, and sea turtles, with their sharp jagged teeth. Others snack on crunchy crabs, shrimp, and lobsters, grinding up the food with their wide flat teeth.

WOW!
A great white shark has the biggest teeth of all sharks. Each tooth is about the same size as your thumb.

▲ Open Wide

Gigantic basking sharks swim along with their mouths wide open. They gulp in vast amounts of water and tiny sea creatures, called plankton, which they eat.

▶ What's Cooking?

A cookie-cutter shark's mouth is shaped like a cookie cutter. This shark sinks its teeth into a passing whale or dolphin, leaving behind a cookie-shaped bite!

◀ Feeding Frenzy

When several sharks dive for the same meal, they can become so excited that they end up tearing one another apart by mistake.

Can You Believe It?

Tiger sharks eat all kinds of garbage! Plastic bags, aluminum foil, wire, coal, wood, leather, empty food cans, car license plates, and wallets have all been found in their stomachs.

I eat anything!

Whale Shark

This huge, spotted creature is a whale shark. It's a
gentle giant that will even let you ride on its back.
Small fish cling to a whale shark's belly and
eat the leftovers that fall out of its mouth.
The fish attach themselves by
using the sticky pads
on their heads.

It's a Laugh!
Why don't sharks
tell lies? Because
they always
tell the tooth!

Q How do sharks keep clean?

A Sharks have their own special cleaning service. Small fish scrub away dead skin and bugs, which they then eat. The fish even clean inside the shark's mouth!

✺ A whale shark is the world's largest fish. It's so huge you could park two school buses on its back.

✺ There are 300 rows of tiny teeth inside a whale shark's mouth. A dental checkup would take a long time!

✺ A whale shark has the biggest mouth of all sharks. It's so huge that you could have a picnic inside it.

Friend or Enemy?

Many people think that sharks are scary monsters out to get them. This is not true. Sharks rarely attack us. Instead, we hurt them. In the past, large sharks were hunted for their meat and as prizes. Luckily, in many countries they are now protected.

Can You Believe It?

Sharks are hunted so that people can make soup from their fins, lipstick from oil inside their bodies, and even necklaces from their teeth.

Waiter, there's a fin in my soup!

▲ A Quick Snap

Scientists help us to become less afraid of sharks. They study sharks carefully and take photos so that we can understand more about the sharks' ways of life.

▼ A Real Sport

A few people still hunt large sharks for sport, but they are now encouraged to release the fish back into the water.

TARPON II

▶ Caught Up

Many harmless sharks are killed in nets each year. The nets are placed in the water near beaches to protect swimmers from more dangerous sharks.

Hammerhead Shark

This weird-looking creature is a hammerhead shark. It gets its name from the shape of its head, which looks like the end of a hammer. A hammerhead shark has an eye and a nostril on each end of the hammer. As it swims, it swings its head from side to side to see and smell in all directions.

It's a Laugh!
Where do sharks go on vacation? Fin-land!

If you stretch your arms out really wide, you could just touch each end of a hammerhead shark's head.

One of a hammerhead shark's favorite foods is a stingray. If you were to eat this fish with its spiky, stinging tail, it would be like munching on a plate of wasps!

Q **Do sharks ever wear sunglasses?**

A Yes! Sharks have their own special sunglasses. In bright light, a thin layer of cells spreads over the sharks' eyes to protect them from the glare of the sun.

When they get really hungry, a few kinds of hammerhead sharks may eat smaller sharks!

Weird and Wonderful

Some of the world's strangest sharks live deep at the bottom of the ocean. There are pink sharks, sharks that shine, and even sharks that can blow up their bodies into big balloons. Other sharks are clever at disguises. They look like patches of sand or seaweed as they lie waiting for their victims.

▶ What Is It?

This creature with a long swordlike mouth is called a saw shark. It sniffs out tasty animals to eat on the seabed. A saw shark looks fierce but it is actually harmless.

Can You Believe It?

When a swell shark spots an enemy, it wedges itself between two rocks. Then it swallows lots of water. This makes its belly grow so big that its enemies cannot pull this shark out.

Help! I'm stuck!

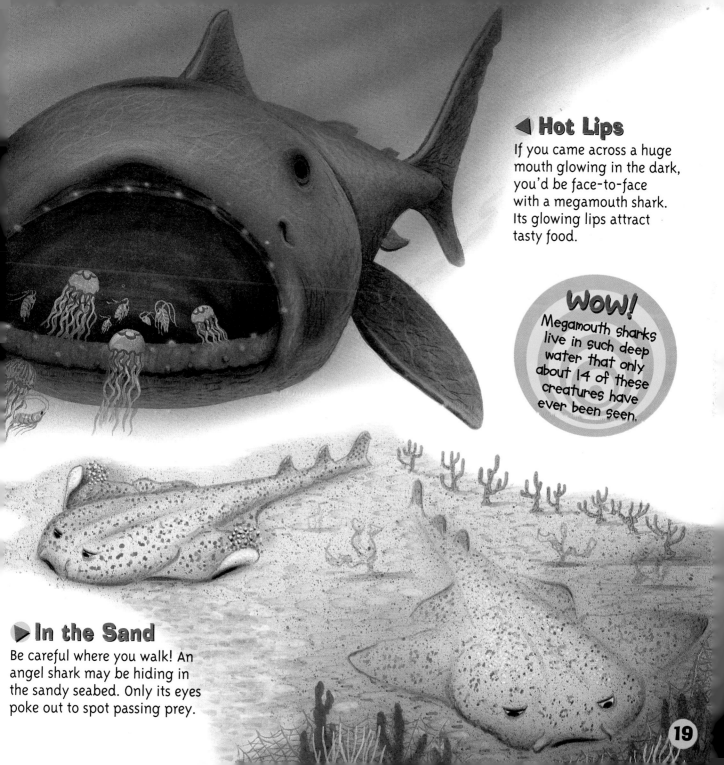

◀ Hot Lips

If you came across a huge mouth glowing in the dark, you'd be face-to-face with a megamouth shark. Its glowing lips attract tasty food.

WOW!

Megamouth sharks live in such deep water that only about 14 of these creatures have ever been seen.

▶ In the Sand

Be careful where you walk! An angel shark may be hiding in the sandy seabed. Only its eyes poke out to spot passing prey.

20

3 Not all sharks are born this way. Dogfish babies grow inside a leathery egg. When the babies are big enough, they nibble their way out.

Hurry up!

All right, I'm coming!

4 As soon as all baby sharks are born, they swim off on their own. If one hangs around its Mom for too long, she might eat it!

That was a lucky escape.

5 For several months, the shark hides in the seagrass and seaweed on the seabed with other baby sharks. Here, it's safe from larger, hungry enemies.

Mmm, no food here.

Your turn!

6 Finally, the young shark heads off to sea. It swims for many years until one day, it meets a mate. They give each other a friendly bite and make lots of babies of their own!

Ouch! I like you!

Puzzle Time

Here are a few puzzles to try. You can look back in the book to help you find the answers.

True or False?

How much do you know about sharks? Answer these true or false questions to find out.

1 When a gray reef shark nods its head, it's about to go to sleep. Hint: Go to page 5.

2 When mako sharks bite boats, they sometimes leave their teeth behind. Hint: Go to page 9.

3 Hammerhead sharks sometimes eat other sharks. Hint: Go to page 17.

4 A whale shark has 200 rows of tiny teeth. Hint: Go to page 13.

Hide-and-Seek

Look carefully at this picture. Can you find two tiger sharks, one angel shark, and one wobbegong lurking in the water?

Close-up

We've zoomed in on these sharks. Can you name them?

1 Hint: Go to page 7.

2 Hint: Go to page 11.

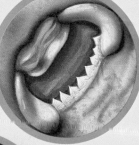

3 Hint: Go to page 10.

Answers

True or False? 1 False, 2 True, 3 True, 4 False

Close-up: 1 tiger shark, 2 cookie-cutter shark, 3 basking shark.

Index

Created by act-two for Scholastic Inc.
Copyright © act-two, 2001.
All rights reserved. Published by Scholastic Inc.
SCHOLASTIC and associated logos are trademarks
and/or registered trademarks of Scholastic Inc.

Main illustrations: Mike Atkinson
Cartoon illustrations: All cartoon illustrations by Simon Clare
except for pp. 20-21 Geo Parkin, p. 23 Alan Rowe
Consultant: Barbara Taylor
Photographs: cover OSF/David B. Fleetham, pp. 4-5 OSF/David B.
Fleetham, pp. 8-9 Stone/Darryl Torckler, pp. 12-13 Bruce Coleman
Inc./Pacific Stock, pp. 16-17 Corbis UK/Amos Nachoum

ISBN 0-439-31710-X

12 11 10 9 8 7 6 5 4 3 2   1 2 3 4 5 6/0

Printed in the U.S.A.

First Scholastic printing, October 2001